Paul Bevan

Harmonies in Japanese Music

Paul Bevan

Harmonies in Japanese Music

ISBN/EAN: 9783337172008

Printed in Europe, USA, Canada, Australia, Japan

Cover: Foto ©Thomas Meinert / pixelio.de

More available books at **www.hansebooks.com**

No. XLI.

armonies

in

Japanese Music.

Privately Printed Opuscula

ISSUED TO MEMBERS OF

THE SETTE OF ODD VOLUMES.

No. XLI.

Harmonies in Japanese Music.

溫故

廬
山
人
書

HARMONIES

IN

Japanese Music.

BY

PAUL BEVAN, M.A.,

READY RECKONER,

TREASURER AND SOMETIME SECRETARY OF YE
SETTE OF ODD VOLUMES.

*Delivered after Dinner at Limmer's Hotel, on the occasion
of the Ladies' Night, Friday, November 1st, 1895.*

LONDON:

Imprynted for the Author at the BEDFORD PRESS,
20 and 21, Bedfordbury, W.C.

MDCCCXCVIII.

On Harmonies in Japanese Music.

MY reasons for introducing such a subject to the notice of the Sette of
Odd Volumes to-night are three in number :

1. The command of His Oddship — HE
   who must be obeyed.

2. The fascination of the subject for me, to
   whom the study of Japanese music
   has always been a source of unmixed
   pleasure.

3. The opportunity of trotting out a hobby
   before one of the most critical and
   distinguished audiences that have ever
   graced our O.V. board.

Under such conditions as these, my subject may appeal to those whose knowledge of Japanese art has been hitherto confined to the fans and bric-à-brac of our universal provider, and even to those to whom the masterpieces of that genius Kōrin are even as caviare, and from whom the delicate handiwork of the versatile Ritsuwō call forth fewer emotions than the sight of black lacquer on the latest pattern S. and T. hansom cab.

It is not my intention, in the short space of time allotted me on a festive occasion of this kind, to make more than a brief incursion into the veiled harmonies that are to be discovered in Japanese music. I dare not lead you into the labyrinths of tone schemes, perturbed harmonics, or phase differences—or still less, introduce you to the hidden mysteries of the missing link between Eastern and Western music, which writers on Oriental music are always endeavouring to, but never do, find.

I speak, too, with diffidence in the presence of the distinguished representative of the Empire of Japan, and possibly of the London correspondent of some technical Japanese music journal.

My object is to interest without instructing you ; and should I succeed in convincing you of anything, it will be due to your own discernment, and not to any theories that I may let loose upon you.

As regards my ☉.♄. Brethren, knowing their critical acumen, I shall later give some examples of Japanese airs harmonised, and let *them* construct theories for themselves.

I should not be surprised if these independent theories were ultimately to tend to a common result. The Latins foresaw the consensus of opinion of the 𝔖𝔢𝔱𝔱𝔢 when they chose the word 𝔒𝔟𝔢𝔰 to indicate creatures who bleat in gregarious (I should say gregorian) chant.

From earliest times Japanese music, like that
of Egypt, from which country every art and
science is supposed to have sprung, was re-
garded as a gift of inspiration, and held in such
esteem that its chief use was in the service to
their deities. Their art had no musical
characters, and their melodies and methods
were transmitted by ear and tradition only, the
priests largely appropriating music to themselves, using it for religious and important state
functions. Gradually it became disseminated
among the people, though one cannot trace in
Japan that laws restricted to their use a limited
number of melodies, which we know was the
case in Egypt. The instruments in vogue in
both countries were very similar as regards
both stringed instruments and those of per-
cussion. The antiphonal mode of singing
existed in both countries; in support of which
statement indisputable evidence as regards
Egypt exists in the works of Ptolemy Phila-

delphus, to say nothing of representations upon Egyptian slabs and tombs ;* and as regards Japan, it is handed down to us by the theatre of the present day.

The Greeks, who got their music from Egypt, used music as an accompaniment to recitation and dialogue ; and the choruses such as those of Aeschylus, the "Wagner" of Hellas, which in the studies of our early days were "skipped" owing to their apparent difficulty, were prominent features in his tragedies, and in those of Sophocles and others. These choruses were difficult of construction, probably owing to their being written to fit the music composed for the early opera-dramas, rather than the converse which now obtains. What the metrical system of the Egyptians and the Greeks was, it is impossible to say, and it is still a disputed point as to whether ἁρμονία or

---

* A questionable example is given on page 42. The words of this are evidently in honour of IBIS or OVES.

συμφωνία meant a complicated system or combination of harmony, or whether it had reference
to a joining together of tetrachords, or groups
of four notes.

In comparing present things with past, in
comparison, say, of the modern German school
of thought with that of the school of Pythagoras,* Lasos and Terpander (600 B.C., or
thereabouts), it is surely no presumption to
assume that where theories were started and
treatises written on such varied subjects as "The

* To Pythagoras and the Greeks it was known that
the notes of the melodic scale corresponded in a curiously
perfect way to certain numerical relations between the
lengths of the stretched strings. (*Brother and Professor
Silvanus P. Thompson*, *D.Sc.*, *M.R.I.*, in his learned
exposition entitled, "The Physical Foundation of
Music," delivered before the Royal Institution of Great
Britain, June 13th, 1890.)
Pythagoras is reported to have invented harmonic
strings through hearing four blacksmiths working with
hammers in harmony, whose weights he found in squares
to be 36, 64, 81, and 144.

Mathematical Precision of the Harmonics," "Sound Pulsations," "The Combination and Cataloguing of Chords," harmony, in the sense we take it—the practice of combining sounds of different pitch—did actually exist in their musical performances.

It does not necessarily follow that the ecclesiastical scales out of which our modern system of harmony was gradually evolved (which scales were the descendants of Greek scales) were a new discovery, for one can point to a race which no one would ever credit with the creation of any new theories in music—I refer to the so-called Scotch, whose soul-stirring, nerve-wrecking, drone-bass was of much greater antiquity; the harmonies of which, no doubt, did more to frighten the legionaries of Agricola or Hadrian than did the kindly offer of their claymore-points or their haggis. I submit that the mere application of this drone-bass in bad fourths or decayed fifths, whichever it is (it depends on the listener's ear) shows a feeling for harmony, and predicts certain issues in the development of harmonic combination which cannot be too easily underrated.

From ancient Greek art to that of Japan is not a far cry, both nations possessing the common characteristics of love of Nature and the picturesque. Though I must admit that Nature evinces no aptitude for music, still, in the words of Whistler, " Nature is creeping up," and may ultimately be trained to recognition of the laws of harmony.

I feel I must justify the aspersion I have just cast upon Dame Nature's musical abilities ; for it must be allowed that certain sounds not due to musical intention convey stray rythmic feeling to the tympanum.*   Those Brethren

* The *Pall Mall Gazette*, in its science columns of a recent issue, tells a story of a tame thrush which escaped after learning " God save the Queen," and returned next year with three companions, who assisted very cleverly in a quartette.

who went down to the sea in a great ship—
that leviathan " La Marguerite," last year—and
did no business in the great waters, will have
a lively recollection of the perfect rhythm with

Without going so far as to believe this entirely, no one
who has listened to the frogs at night, or to the chirping
of the too vociferous cicala, can doubt that the animal
world possesses instances of the choral instinct. An
inhabitant of the mountains of North Carolina writes
to *Science* as if such instances were unknown, and
describes a nocturnal concert of that interesting "bug"
known as the katydid. When these insects elect to sing
in the branches, sleep goes from the home. Wearily
the householder lies awake for eight hours at a stretch,
taking note of this strange music. It begins at sun-
down with a few scattered scrapings of the leaders,
and then the orchestra settles in, dividing into two
vast bodies which answer each other in antiphonies
which sound to the distracted ears like the rhythm of
a cross-saw. A gust of wind upsets the concert, and the
scattered notes begin again, the leading voices being
the more pronounced, and the answering note being
from one to five tones lower. North Carolina must be
a bad place to sleep in during the time of the "New
Talk."

which the sad sea waves broke over and against the good ship's sides.

But it is not only in Nature that we occasionally recognise a well-meant attempt at musical sounds, but even in the apparently most unlikely works of man : *e.g.*, in the cadence of the *obligato* supplied by the *andantissimo* rumbling of a South-Eastern Railway express, crawling to the south, which, taken of course in the slowest time, and forty minutes behind that, vividly recalls the " Brek-kek-keks " of "The Frogs " of Aristophanes.

To revert to pre-railway times :

It is easy to trace the opera-dramas in Japan and Greece, starting from divine inspiration, to finally develope into opera-dramas of hero life, the poets of both countries writing their tragedies in verse whereby to gain the power of expressing great thoughts with the greatest amount of dignity that language can command, their verses being sung in order that they may be invested with a deeper pathos than the most careful form of ordinary declamation can reach.

The earliest records of a *Conservatoire* in Japan date from about the early part of the VIIIth Century, when the Emperor Mommū established something of this kind for his household in order that Chinese dance music might be learnt, performed, and appreciated ; a *Conservatoire* which has lasted into the present day, some of the present dancers being lineal descendants of those that performed before the Emperor mentioned.

Chinese music acted like the advent of Italian music in England in the eighteenth century : it created a fashion for foreign, to the detriment of native, art.

The old *Kāgŭra* ceremony, however, outlived these Chinese innovations ; a natural music resulted, fostered by a skilful adaptation of the foreign instrument to the Japanese *Biwa* or lute.

B

The performances of dances soon developed into the *Utai* or song-dramas which, originally composed by the priests of Buddha, outgrew their original scope, and became operettas containing what are now known as "topical allusions" to a marked extent.

By the commencement of the XVIIth Century, licensed theatrical performances were in full swing, chiefly in the form of opera-dramas.

The orchestra to these was composed of two *samisens* or three-stringed lutes, one flute, big, side, and shoulder drums, and two reciters : in other words, the *Kapelle* and *chorus* of the ancient Greek theatre.*

* Du côté opposé à l'orchestre . . . se tient le *choeur* . . . Son rôle correspond assez exactement à celui du choeur de la tragédie grecque : il tient cependant plus de place dans le drame japonais.   Il represente le bon sens populaire et la morale commune ; mais il explique surtout le dévellopement du drame ; il raconte au besoin ce qui se passe hors de la scène, et dévoile les sentiments inte-

The musical scale in Japan consists of a minor scale with a flat second, *e.g.*,

$$C\sharp \ D \ E \ F\sharp \ G\sharp \ A\sharp \ B\sharp \ C\sharp.$$

This scale may not be the same as our system as far as vibrations are concerned, but it is identical with our diatonic and chromatic scale. The Japanese know naught of acoustics, yet the result of their harmonies is the same.

"Our harmonies are based on certain harmonic considerations. Were the Japanese accustomed to hear our harmonised themes, they would probably recognise the laws which underlie the construction of melody itself, and their music would show more the effect of this wider knowledge." In other words, their science has given them the natural notes

rieurs des personnages.—*Le Théatre Japonais* (Bibliothèque Orientale, No. LXIII.), par A. Lequeux ; Paris, 1889.

Pythagoras employed—a systematic sequence
of notes—while their instinct has led them (in
the words of Mr. Piggott*) into a sequence
which is the sequence of the West—a curious
divergence from the Chinese scale which may

* " The Music and Musical Instruments of Japan, by
Mr. F. T. Piggott, Honorary Member Japan Society ;
with notes by T. L. Southgate." Mr. Piggott, in a
paper on the "Japanese Musical Scale," read before
the Japan Society subsequent to the publication of his
above-mentioned exhaustive work, and to the date of
my paper, disposes of his would-be critics successfully
enough.

Admitting that the character of the music of the
Japanese is entirely pentatonic, he maintains that their
scale, as instanced by the principal tunings of the *Koto*,
is identical with the European diatonic scale.

He thus concludes a remarkable paper :— " The
Japanese *Koto* is an equal-temperament instrument, its
notes being identical with those of the equal-temperament
piano ; only Japan did not borrow this from the West—
it was in use by Yatsuhashi, the inventor of the *Koto*,
rather more than 120 years before Sebastian Bach
wrote his Preludes and Fugues for the Well-Tempered
Clavier."

possibly be attributed to the mixture of various strains in the Japanese race.

An illustration from the Delphian hymn to Apollo, followed by the national anthem of Japan in unison, will show what I mean.

[The orchestra here played—

      1. Ode to Apollo.

      2. Kimiga-yo.]

There can be no doubt that the harmonies latent though displayed in Japanese music are better shown in their *samisen* music than in that of the *koto* (or Japanese zither), and I further assert that their harmonies are not only hinted at but ready for European treatment.

One striking analogy as regards the harmonies of Japan and of the West is the similarity of scheme followed in the opera-dramas of Japan and the opera - dramas of Richard Wagner. I am myself a witness to the fact that in the opera-drama performed to this day in Japan, a leading motive, the very counterpart of the Wagnerian *leit-motiv*, runs through the whole production.* This is especially noticeable in the numerous Japanese hero-plays based on the peculiarly Greek idea of inexorable Destiny overtaking the hero, and making itself felt throughout by premonitory musical expressions, similar to the warning whisper of the *Waldvogel* to *Siegfried* in the Bayreuth Master's immortal work. A striking example of this I have called *Sayonara* (Farewell).

The examples of Japanese music which have just been so ably performed by the only

* Elle (la musique) joue presque sans discontinuer, accompagnant le dialogue d'une mélodie grave ou sautillante, triste ou gaie, discrète ou emportée, sourde ou bruyante, autant que possible à l'unisson morale de la situation.

Cette mélodie sert à réprésenter aussi le murmure de la nature ; elle cherche des harmonies imitatives, devient tour à tour tempête, zéphir, tonnerre, pluie, cascade, courant léger, etc., etc.—*Le Théatre Japonais ;* A. Lequeux.

orchestra in this country which has been trained to produce them, will have, I trust, sufficed to convince you that, strange and weird as these melodies may have appeared to your unaccustomed ears, there is in all of them a substratum of musical truth, that is to say, a proper sequence of sounds, as they appear to me, capable of affording pleasure to any ear Eastern or Western.

At all events, I think it not unworthy of our Sette that it should have devoted some time this evening to its faithful servant's attempt to make it acquainted with the music which has enchanted for so many centuries the courts and peoples of the Land of the Rising Sun.

Sayonara.

DISCUSSION.

The PRESIDENT asked the *Portreeve* to move a vote of thanks to the *Ready Reckoner* for the above paper, which that worthy did in his invariably gracious manner.

The *Alchemist* having seconded the vote, the *Interpreter* made a few remarks on the difficulty experienced by Japanese in following their own melodies as performed by foreigners.

His Excellency the Japanese Minister, Mr. T. Kato, followed, supporting the *Interpreter's* views ; he could follow the airs more easily when performed by Japanese rather than by English orchestras, although he had no doubt the airs imported by the *Ready Reckoner* were genuine, and made in Japan.

The *Playwright* asked if the harmonies were actually Japanese, or the tone-schemes of the *Ready Reckoner* himself.

The *Ready Reckoner*, in reply, disclaimed the authorship of the harmonies in question ; and, referring to his paper, maintained that these were discoverable to those who chose to study the subject.

The *Pilgrim* supported the *Ready Reckoner*, more especially as to his insistance on Japanese *leit-motivs*.

The *Mechanic* asked His Oddship to request the *Ready Reckoner* to print, publish, and issue to the 𝕾𝖊𝖙𝖙𝖊 his paper as an opusculum, if possible with the airs themselves (in European notation) that had been performed that night, together with the discussion thereon.

The PRESIDENT put the vote of thanks to the meeting, and it was carried by acclamation; the 𝕾𝖊𝖙𝖙𝖊 and the guests settling down to a delightful demonstration by the *Magnetizer* on " Rotatory Magnetism."

C

EXAMPLES

CHIEFLY FROM THE

MIYAKO-DORI COLLECTION * OF JAPANESE MELODIES.

---

* MIYAKO-DORI: Japanese Melodies, collected and arranged for the Voice or Pianoforte, by Paul Bevan, M.A., Hon. Treasurer of the Japan Society, London. English Lyrics by Antonia Williams. With Illustrations in the Text from drawings by Hokusai (*d.* 1849), Kuniyoshi (*d.* 1861), and other famous Japanese Artists. Ent. Sta. Hall. London: Novello, Ewer and Co.

(27)

D

Kimi=Ga=Yo.

REIGN OF MY SOVEREIGN.

JAPANESE NATIONAL ANTHEM.

Largo.

May our Emperor's reign en - dure, Stand increas-ing -
Just as leaves by autumn sown, Red and fair to

- ly se - cure, .. True and fast shall it last
earth are blown, Just as these nev - er cease,

Till a mil - lion years have passed; Thus shall he
Year by year to shed their peace; Thus shall he

prais - ed be to E - ter - ni - ty.
reign to see E - ter - ni - ty.

Yosakoi.

Vain the dream where-in I thought to see thee, Vain the dream where-in thine arms en -

-twined me, Hope there is none, and vain the thought of

heav'n, To .. dark - ness given.

Manzai.

WISHING YOU TEN THOUSAND YEARS HAPPINESS.

Allegro molto e con brio.

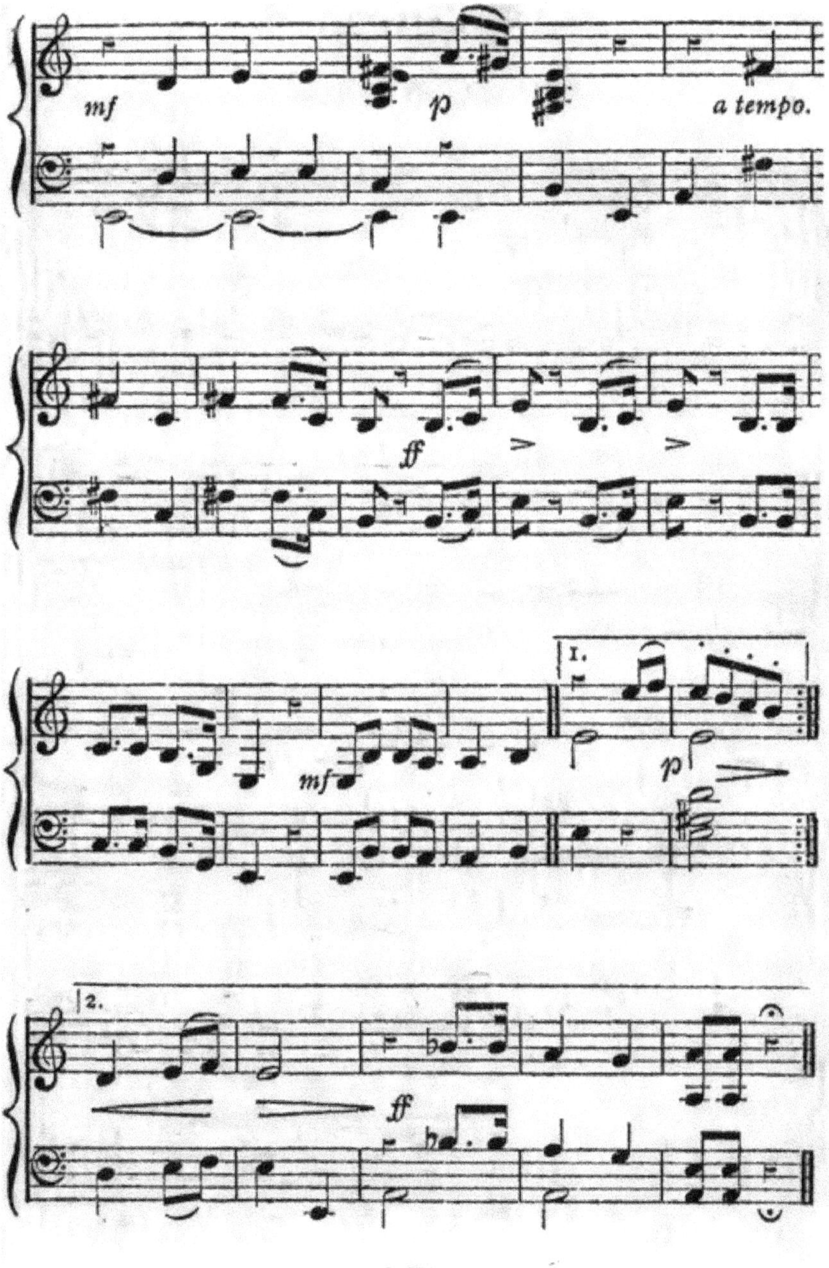
mf
p
a tempo.
ff
mf
1.
p
2.
ff

Sakura.

CHERRY BLOSSOMS.

Hime=Matsu.

LITTLE FIR TREE.

Chô Chô Tombo.

BUTTERFLY! DRAGONFLY!

Chô, Chô, Tom - bo, ni Ki - ri - gi - ri - su.

Ya - ma - dé. . . . na - ku . . Mu - si,

Matsu-mu-si, Su - zu -mu - si, Ku - tsu -wa - mu - si.

Miya Sama.

WAR SONG OF THE IMPERIAL ARMY (1867—8).

Mi - ya Sa - ma Mi - ya Sa - ma O - Um - a - no
A - re wa cho te - ki Se - i - bats

may - e - ni   Pi - ra Pi - ra   su - ru no - wa
seyo   tono   nis - hi - ki   no   mi - ha - ta wo

ff CHORUS.

Nan   ja - i - na?   To - ko   to - ni - a,   re
Shi - ra - nai - ka?   To - ko   to - ni - a,   re

to - ni - a   re - na.
to - ni - a   re - na.

(39)

Sayonara.

FAREWELL.

cres - - - cen - - - do.

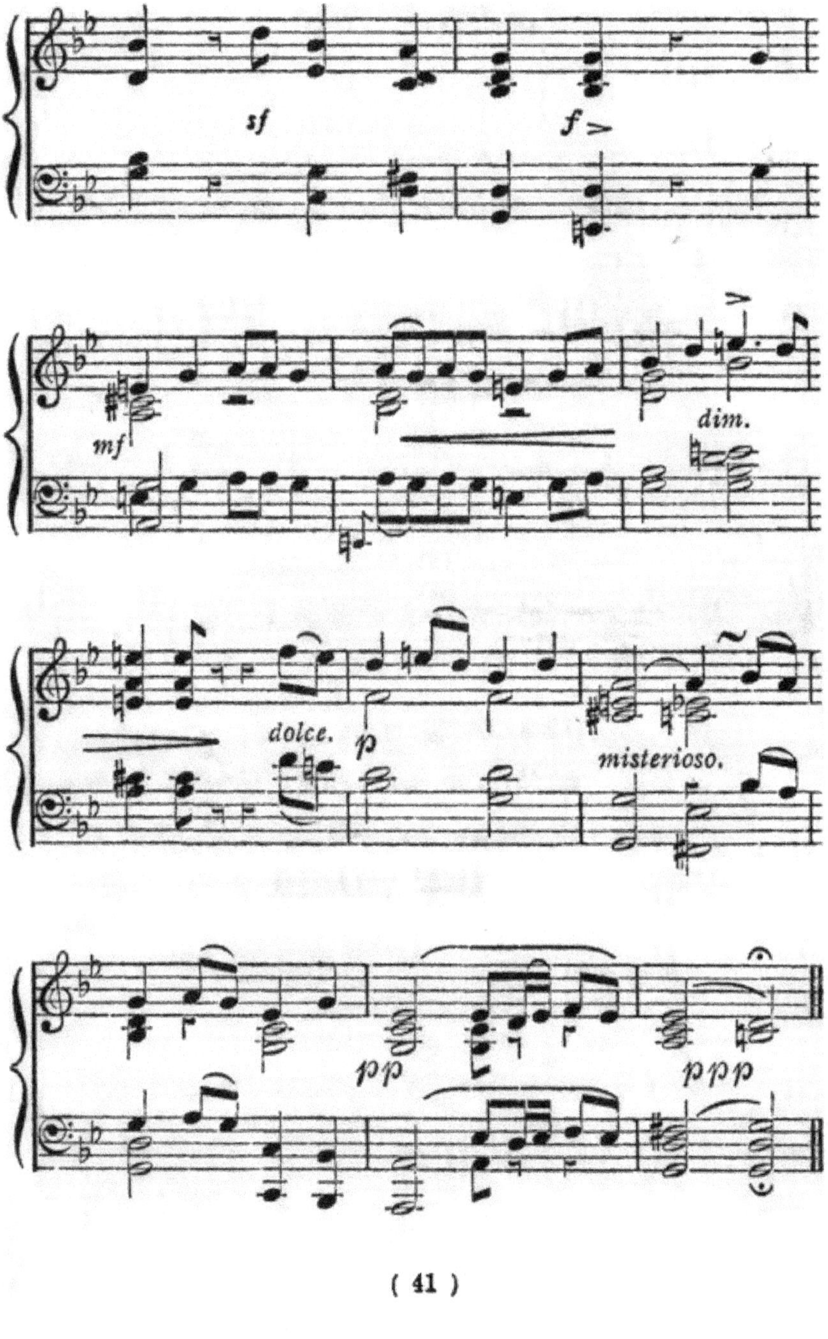
sf
f >
mf
dim.
dolce.
p
misterioso.
pp
ppp

Ancient Egyptian Hymn.

IN HONOUR OF IBIS OR OVES.

ΟΔΔ ΥΕΡΙ ΟΔΔ

ΕΥΜΑΤΑ ΚΙΤΩΗΑ

Ρ' ΟΔΔ, ΧΡΟΝΟC

ΚΑΤΑΛΟΞ' ΑΛΗΘΩC.

CΤΕΦΑΝΩΜΕΝΟC.

APPENDIX.

Diversity of opinion amongst musical critics is shewn in the following extracts from the Press :—

The Morning.—"His aim has been to reproduce as nearly as possible on a keyed instrument, like the piano, the exact effect of traditional Japanese strains. Accordingly, certain of the tunes will seem most unconventional to European purists, while all will be found to have been treated with great taste. A skilful compromise has, in fact, been achieved between the harmony of the original airs and that which will render them intelligible to Western ears. Mr. Bevan has done his work well."

Public Opinion—Leeds Mercury.—"Quite of unusual interest."

Lady's World.—" Monotonous and doleful."

Illustrated London News.—" Exceedingly interesting."

Musical Times.—"'Yosakoi' is a taking piece, the refinement of which is not restricted to the words, and it was ably rendered by Mr. Charles Phillips."

Westminster Gazette.—"Although the arrangement is as a rule decidedly European in character, the melodies are strikingly original and for the most part of great beauty."

Science and Art.—"Japanese art has long been appreciated, but it has been left for Mr. Bevan to introduce Japanese music. The melodies, though somewhat strange to English ears, and quite beyond just rendering by English instruments, are yet most fascinating."

The Queen.—" Mr. Charles Phillips, the baritone, sang with marked fervour . . . an interesting Japanese Love Song, 'Yosakoi," arranged by Mr. Paul Bevan."

The Times.—"A remarkably attractive publication. The difficult task of arranging them for European hearers has been, on the whole, very successfully accomplished. The best specimen is perhaps the plaintive 'Yosakoi,' which might very well find a place in concert programmes, so nearly does it conform to Western tonalities."

The Queen.—"Charming little songs, that will stir heartaches in those who have lounged away delicious hours in far-away Japanese tea houses."

Puddleborough Weekly Guardian. — " Mr. Bevan has done a real service to the cause of music. This sort of thing should be worked off in front of an Asylum for the Deaf and Dumb."

Globe.—" Japanese music seems to have made a great advance just at present in its interest for Western ears."

Daily Chronicle.—" Still one more Japanese book! This time on the rather unpromising subject of Japanese music."

Quarterly Musical Review.—"A more artistic publication has rarely been met with. Apart from the interest which the quaint and beautiful melodies cannot fail to excite, there is added the further charm of picturesque design and finish. Mr. Bevan has fulfilled his task with great care in collecting his materials from their original sources. The harmonies are well chosen, and the accompaniments arranged with discretion."

The Studio.—"Arranged for the voice and pianoforte with excellent discretion. It would have been so easy to overload the melody itself by introducing harmony which is practically unknown to the Japanese, and so to have lost the peculiar character of the crisp strident tune, that the happy reticence deserves full praise. The 'Sayonara' an exquisitely plaintive strain of farewell, presents a new effect in tone-scheme, and the 'Manzai' is a study in the unexpected."

London and China Telegraph.—"If you are familiar with the National Anthem of Japan, or the popular air known as 'Chon Kina,' you will certainly recognise them, but they will not appear exactly the same. This, we would hasten to say, is not due to any defects on the part of Mr. Bevan, but to difficulties which may be stated as insurmountable."

Aus Fremden Zungen (STUTTGART). — "Die Kunst und das Kunstgewerbe Japans erfreuen sich einer von Jahr zu Jahr steigenden Anerkennung, so dass sie sogar Einfluss auf den europäischen Geschmack gewonnen haben. Fast noch unbekannt ist aber die japanische Musik, u.s.w."

Envoi.

Des Wissens bar,
　　Doch des Wunsches voll!

Brünnhilde.
(*Wagner's* "*Götterdämmerung.*")

(46)

"There is Divinity in Odd Numbers."—SHAKESPEARE.

Ɏe Sette of ɏe Odd Volumes.

(November, 1895.)

With the Titles, Offices, and Addresses of the Members.

†1878. BERNARD QUARITCH, *Librarian.*
  15, Piccadilly, W.
    PRESIDENT, 1878, 1879, and 1882.

†1878. W. MORT THOMPSON, *Historiographer.*
  16, Carlyle Square, Chelsea, S.W.
  VICE-PRESIDENT, 1882 ; PRESIDENT, 1883.

†1878. CHARLES W. H. WYMAN, *Typographer.*
  103, King Henry's Road, Primrose Hill, N.W.
    VICE-PRESIDENT, 1878 and 1879 ;
      PRESIDENT, 1880.

† Original Member.

F

†1878. ALFRED J. DAVIES, *Attorney-General.*
Fairlight, Uxbridge Road, Ealing, W.
VICE-PRESIDENT, 1881 ; SECRETARY, 1884 ;
PRESIDENT, 1887.

1878. Alderman SIR GEORGE R. TYLER, BART.
(Lord Mayor, 1893-94), *Stationer.*
17, Penywern Road, S.W.
VICE-PRESIDENT, 1886.

1879. T. C. VENABLES, *Antiquary.*
9, Marlborough Place, N.W.
PRESIDENT, 1888.

1879. JAMES ROBERTS BROWN, F.R.G.S., *Alchymist.*
44, Tregunter Road, South Kensington, S.W.
SECRETARY, 1880 ; VICE-PRESIDENT, 1883 ;
PRESIDENT, 1885.

1880. BURNHAM W. HORNER, *Organist.*
29, Redcliffe Gardens, S.W.
VICE-PRESIDENT, 1889.

1883. HENRY GEORGE LILEY, *Art Director.*
Radnor House, Radnor Place, Hyde Park, W.

† Original Member.

1883. GEORGE CHARLES HAITÉ, F.L.S., R.B.A.,
Art Critic.

Ormsby Lodge, The Avenue, Bedford Park, W.

VICE-PRESIDENT, 1887 ; PRESIDENT, 1891.

1884. WILFRID BALL, R.P.E., *Painter-Etcher.*
4, Albemarle Street, W.

MASTER OF CEREMONIES, 1890; VICE-
PRESIDENT, 1891.

1884. DANIEL W. KETTLE, F.R.G.S., *Cosmographer.*

Hayes Common, near Beckenham, Kent.

SECRETARY, 1886.

1886. CHARLES HOLME, F.L.S., *Pilgrim.*
The Red House, Bexley Heath, Kent.

SECRETARY, 1887 ; PRESIDENT, 1890.

1886. FREDK. H. GERVIS, M.R.C.S.,*Apothecary.*
𝔓𝔯𝔢𝔰𝔦𝔡𝔢𝔫𝔱.

1, Fellows Road, Haverstock Hill, N.W.

1887. JOHN W. BRODIE-INNES, *Master of the
Rolls.*

15, Royal Circus, Edinburgh.

SECRETARY, 1888.

1887. HENRY MOORE, R.A., *Ancient Mariner*.
Collingham, Maresfield Gardens, N.W.

1887. JAMES ORROCK, R.I., *Connoisseur*.
48, Bedford Square, W.C.

1888. ALFRED EAST, R.P.E. *Landscape Painter*.
4, Grove End Road, St. John's Wood.
VICE-PRESIDENT, 1893.

1888. WALTER HAMILTON, *Parodist*.
𝔐aster of 𝔈eremonies.
Ellarbee, Elms Road, Clapham Common, S.W.
(Keeper of the Archives.)

1888. ALEXANDER T. HOLLINGSWORTH,
Artificer.
2, Belsize Grove, N.W.
VICE-PRESIDENT, 1890 ; PRESIDENT, 1893.

1888. JOHN LANE, *Bibliographer*.
G 1, The Albany.
SECRETARY, 1890 ; MASTER OF CEREMONIES,
1891.

Supplemental Odd Volumes.

1888. JOHN TODHUNTER, M.D., *Playwright*.
Orchard Croft, The Orchard, Bedford Park, W.
SECRETARY, 1892.

1889. FRANCIS ELGAR, LL.D., F.R.S.E., *Ship-wright*.
18, York Terrace, Regent's Park, N.W.
PRESIDENT, 1894.

1889. WILLIAM MANNING, *Seer*.
21, Redcliffe Gardens, S.W.
SECRETARY, 1891 ; VICE-PRESIDENT, 1894.

1890. SILVANUS P. THOMPSON, D.Sc., F.R.S., *Magnetiser*.
Morland, Chislett Road, N.W.

1890. CONRAD W. COOKE, M. INST. E. E., *Mechanick*.
"Rothley," Macaulay Road, Clapham Common, S.W.
SECRETARY, 1893.

1891. CHARLES PLUMPTRE JOHNSON, *Clerke at Law.*

            Vice=President.

8, Savile Row, W.

1891. FREDERIC VILLIERS, *War Correspondent.*
Mashrabeyah, 65, Chancery Lane, W.C.

1892. MARCUS B. HUISH, LL.B., *Arts-man.*
21, Essex Villas, Phillimore Gardens, W.

1892. W. WILSEY MARTIN, *Laureate.*
15, Delamere Terrace, W.

    MASTER OF THE CEREMONIES, 1894.

1892. FREDERIC YORK POWELL, *Ignoramus.*
The Corner, Priory Road, Bedford Park, W.

1892. ERNEST CLARKE, M.A., F.S.A., *Yeoman.*
13a, Hanover Square, W.

    MASTER OF CEREMONIES, 1893.

1892. PAUL BEVAN, M.A., F.C.A., *Ready Reckoner.*

        Secretary and Treasurer.

Leadenhall Buildings, E.C.

       (SECRETARY, 1894.)

1893. RICHARD LE GALLIENNE, *Rhymer.*
Mulberry Cottage, Boston Road, New Brentford, Middlesex.

1894. T. REGINALD CLEAVER, *Illustrator.*
22, Bolton Studios, Redcliffe Road, S.W.

1894. PROF. WILLIAM ANDERSON, F.R.C.S., *Chirurgeon.*
2, Harley Street, Cavendish Square, W.

1894. HENRY B. WHEATLEY, F.S.A., *Recorder.*
𝕬𝖚𝖉𝖎𝖙𝖔𝖗.
2, Oppidans Road, Primrose Hill, N.W.

1894. ALDERMAN SIR STUART KNILL, BART., LL.D. (Lord Mayor, 1892-3), *Portreeve.*
Fresh Wharf, London Bridge, E.C.

1895. CAPT. SIDNEY EARDLEY-WILMOT, R.N., *Boatswain.*
23, Cranley Gardens, S.W.

1895. CHARLES ST. JOHN HORNBY, *Chapman,*
186, Strand, W.C.

𝔒.𝔙.

A BIBLIOGRAPHY

OF THE

PRIVATELY PRINTED OPUSCULA

Issued to the Members of the Sette of Odd Volumes.

"Books that can be held in the hand, and carried to the fireside, are the best after all."—*Samuel Johnson.*

"The writings of the wise are the only riches our posterity cannot squander."—*Charles Lamb.*

1. B. Q.

A Biographical and Bibliographical Fragment. 22 pages. Presented on November the 5th, 1880, by His Oddship C. W. H. WYMAN. 1st Edition limited to 25 copies. (Subsequently enlarged to 50 copies.)

2. Glossographia Anglicana.

By the late J. TROTTER BROCKETT, F.S.A., London and Newcastle, author of "Glossary of North Country Words," to which is prefixed a Biographical Sketch of the Author by FREDERICK BLOOMER. (pp. 94.) Presented on July the 7th, 1882, by His Oddship BERNARD QUARITCH.
Edition limited to 150 copies.

3. Ye Boke of Ye Odd Volumes,

from 1878 to 1883. Carefvlly *Compiled* and painsfvlly *Edited* by ye vnworthy Historiographer to ye Sette, *Brother* and *Vice-President* WILLIAM MORT THOMPSON, and produced by ye

order and at ye charges of Hys Oddship ye President and
Librarian of ye Sette, Bro. BERNARD QUARITCH. (pp. 136.)
Presented on April 13th, 1883, by His Oddship BERNARD
QUARITCH.   Edition limited to 150 copies.

4. Love's Garland ;

Or Posies for Rings, Hand-kerchers, & Gloves, and such pretty
Tokens that Lovers send their Loves.   London, 1674.   A
Reprint. And Ye Garland of Ye Odd Volumes. (pp. 102.)
Presented on October the 12th, 1883, by Bro. JAMES ROBERTS
BROWN.   Edition limited to 250 copies.

5. Queen Anne Musick.

A brief Accompt of ye genuine Article, those who performed
ye same, and ye Masters in ye facultie. From 1702 to 1714.
(pp. 40.) Presented on July the 13th, 1883, by Bro. BURNHAM
W. HORNER.   Edition limited to 100 copies.

6. A Very Odd Dream.

Related by His Oddship, W. M. THOMPSON, President of the
Sette of Odd Volumes, at the Freemasons' Tavern, Great
Queen Street, on June 1st, 1883. (pp. 26.) Presented on
July the 13th, 1883, by His Oddship W. MORT THOMPSON.
                               Edition limited to 250 copies.

7. Codex Chiromantiae.

Being a compleate Manualle of ye Science and Arte of
Expoundynge ye Past, ye Presente, ye Future, and ye
Charactere, by ye Scrutinie of ye Hande, ye Gestures thereof,
and ye Chirographie. *Codicillus I.*—CHIROGNOMY. (pp. 118.)
Presented on November 2nd, 1883, by Bro. ED. HERON-ALLEN.
                               Edition limited to 133 copies.

8. Intaglio Engraving : Past and Present.

An Address by Bro. EDWARD RENTON, delivered at the Freemasons' Tavern, Great Queen Street, on December 5th, 1884.
(pp. 74.) Presented to the Sette by His Oddship EDWARD
F. WYMAN.   Edition limited to 200 copies.

9. The Rights, Duties, Obligations, and Advantages of Hospitality.

An Address by Bro. CORNELIUS WALFORD, F.I.A., F.S.S.,
F.R.Hist.Soc., Barrister-at-Law, Master of the Rolls in the

Sette of Odd Volumes, delivered at the Freemasons' Tavern, Great Queen Street, on Friday, February 5th, 1885. (pp. 72.) Presented to the Sette by His Oddship EDWARD F. WYMAN.
Edition limited to 133 copies.

10. "Pens, Ink, and Paper:" a Discourse upon Caligraphy.

The Implements and Practice of Writing, both Ancient and Modern, with Curiosa, and an Appendix of famous English Penmen, by Bro. DANIEL W. KETTLE, F.R.G.S., Cosmographer; delivered at the Freemasons' Tavern, Great Queen Street, on Friday, November 6th, 1885. (pp. 104.) Presented to the Sette on January 8th, 1886, by Bro. DANIEL W. KETTLE.
Edition limited to 233 copies.

11. On Some of the Books for Children of the Last Century.

With a few Words on the Philanthropic Publisher of St. Paul's Churchyard. A Paper read at a Meeting of the Sette of Odd Volumes by Brother CHARLES WELSH, Chapman of the Sette, at the Freemasons' Tavern, on Friday, the 8th day of January, 1886. (pp. 108.) Presented to the Sette by Bro. CHARLES WELSH.
Edition limited to 250 copies.

12. Frost Fairs on the Thames.

An Address by Bro. EDWARD WALFORD, M.A., Rhymer to the Sette of the Odd Volumes, delivered at Willis's Rooms, on Friday, December 3rd, 1886. (pp. 76.) Presented to the Sette by His Oddship GEORGE CLULOW.
Edition limited to 133 copies.

13. On Coloured Books for Children.

By Bro. CHARLES WELSH, Chapman to the Sette. Read before the Sette, at Willis's Rooms, on Friday, the 6th May, 1887. With a Catalogue of the Books Exhibited, (pp. 60.) Presented to the Sette by Bro. JAMES ROBERTS BROWN.
Edition limited to 255 copies.

14. A Short Sketch of Liturgical History and Literature.

Illustrated by Examples Manuscript and Printed. A Paper read at a Meeting of the Sette of Odd Volumes by Bro.

BERNARD QUARITCH, Librarian and First President of the Sette, at Willis's Rooms, on Friday, June 10th, 1887. (pp. 86.) Presented to the Sette by Bro. BERNARD QUARITCH.

15. Cornelius Walford : In Memoriam.

By his Kinsman, EDWARD WALFORD, M.A., Rhymer to the Sette of Odd Volumes. Read before the Sette at Willis's Rooms, on Friday, October 21st, 1887. (pp. 60.) Presented to the Sette by Bro. EDWARD WALFORD, M.A.
Edition limited to 255 copies.

16. The Sweating Sickness.

By FREDERICK H. GERVIS, M.R.C.S., Apothecary to the Sette of Odd Volumes, delivered at Willis's Rooms, on Friday, November 4th, 1887. (pp. 48.) Presented to the Sette by Bro. FRED. H. GERVIS.   Edition limited to 133 copies.

17. New Year's Day in Japan.

By Bro. CHARLES HOLME, Pilgrim of the Sette of Odd Volumes. Read before the Sette at Willis's Rooms, on Friday, January 6th, 1888. (pp. 46.) Presented to the Sette by Bro. CHARLES HOLME.   Edition limited to 133 copies.

18. Ye Seconde Boke of Ye Odd Volumes,

from 1883 to 1888. Carefvlly *Compiled* and painsfvlly *Edited* by ye vnworthy Historiographer to ye Sette, BRO. WILLIAM MORT THOMPSON, and produced by ye order and at ye charges of ye Sette. (pp. 157.)   Edition limited to 115 copies.

19. Repeats and Plagiarisms in Art, 1888.

By Bro. JAMES ORROCK, R.I., Connoisseur to the Sette of Odd Volumes. Read before the Sette at Willis's Rooms, St. James's, on Friday, January 4th, 1889. (pp. 33.) Presented to the Sette by Bro. JAMES ORROCK, R.I.
Edition limited to 133 copies.

20. How Dreams Come True.

A Dramatic Sketch by Bro. J. TODHUNTER, Bard of the Sette of Odd Volumes. Performed at a Conversazione of the Sette at the Grosvenor Gallery, on Thursday, July 17th, 1890. (pp. 46.) Presented to the Sette by His Oddship Bro. CHARLES HOLME.
Edition limited to 600 copies.

21. The Drama in England during the Last Three Centuries.

By Bro. WALTER HAMILTON, F.R.G.S., Parodist to the Sette of Odd Volumes. Read before the Sette at Limmer's Hotel, on Wednesday, January 8th, 1890. (pp. 80.) Presented to the Sette by Bro. WALTER HAMILTON.

Edition limited to 201 copies.

22. Gilbert, of Colchester.

By Bro. SILVANUS P. THOMPSON, D.Sc., B.A., Magnetizer to the Sette of Odd Volumes. Read before the Sette at Limmer's Hotel, on Friday, July 4th, 1890. (pp. 63.) Presented to the Sette by Bro. SILVANUS P. THOMPSON.

Edition limited to 249 copies.

23. Neglected Frescoes in Northern Italy.

By Bro. DOUGLAS H. GORDON. Remembrancer to the Sette of Odd Volumes. Read before the Sette at Limmer's Hotel, on Friday, December 6th, 1889. (pp. 48.) Presented to the Sette by Bro. DOUGLAS H. GORDON.

Edition limited to 133 copies.

24. Recollections of Robert-Houdin.

By Bro. WILLIAM MANNING, Seer to the Sette of Odd Volumes. Delivered at a Meeting of the Sette held at Limmer's Hotel, on Friday, December 7th, 1890. (pp. 81.) Presented to the Sette by Bro. WILLIAM MANNING.

Edition limited to 205 copies.

25. Scottish Witchcraft Trials.

By Bro. J. W. BRODIE-INNES, Master of the Rolls to the Sette of Odd Volumes. Read before the Sette at a Meeting held at Limmer's Hotel, on Friday, November 7th, 1890. (pp. 66.) Presented to the Sette by Bro. ALDERMAN TYLER.

Edition limited to 245 copies.

26. Blue and White China.

By Bro. ALEXANDER T. HOLLINGSWORTH, Artificer to the Sette of Odd Volumes. Delivered at a Meeting of the Sette held at Limmer's Hotel, on Friday, February 6th, 1891. (pp. 70.) Presented to the Sette by Bro. ALEXANDER T. HOLLINGSWORTH.

Edition limited to 245 copies.

27. Reading a Poem.

A Forgotten Sketch by WM. M. THACKERAY. Communicated by Bro. CHAS. PLUMPTRE JOHNSON (Clerke-atte-Lawe to the Sette of Odd Volumes), to the Sette at Limmer's Hotel, on Friday, May 1st, 1891. (pp. xi. and 66.) Psesented to the Sette by Bro. CHAS. PLUMPTRE JOHNSON.

Edition limited to 321 copies.

28. The Ballades of a Blasé Man,

to which are added some Rondeaux of his Rejuvenescence, laboriously constructed by the Necromancer to the Sette of Odd Volumes. (pp. 88.) Presented to the Sette by Bro. EDWARD HERON-ALLEN, in October, 1891.

Edition limited to 99 copies.

29. Automata, Old and New.

By Bro. CONRAD W. COOKE, Mechanick to the Sette of Odd Volumes. Read before the Sette at a Meeting held at Limmer's Hotel, on Friday, November 6th, 1891. (pp. 118.) Presented to the Sette by Bro. CONRAD W. COOKE.

Edition limited to 255 copies.

30. Ye Magick Mirrour of Old Japan.

By Bro. SILVANUS P. THOMPSON, D.Sc., F.R.S., Magnetizer to the Sette of Odd Volumes. Read before the Sette at Limmer's Hotel, on Friday, December 2nd, 1892. (pp. 63.) Presented to the Sette by Bro. SILVANUS P. THOMPSON.

Edition limited to 97 copies.

31. Life and Works of Dr. Arne, 1710 to 1778.

By Bro. BURNHAM W. HORNER, Organist to the Sette of Odd Volumes. Delivered at a Meeting of the Sette held at Limmer's Hotel, Friday, May 5th, 1893. (pp. viii. and 43.) Printed by the order and at the charge of the Sette.

Edition limited to 155 copies.

32. Our Noses.

By Bro. WILLIAM WILSEY MARTIN, Laureate to the Sette of Odd Volumes. Delivered at a Meeting of the Sette, held at Limmer's Hotel, on Friday, November 3rd, 1893. (pp. 103.)

Edition limited to 199 copies.

33. Ships, Old and New.

By Bro. FRANCIS ELGAR, LL.D., F.R.S., Shipwright to the
Sette of Odd Volumes. Read at a Meeting of the Sette held
at Limme·'s Hotel, on Friday, January 12th, 1894. (pp. 92.)
Presented to the Sette by Bro. FRANCIS ELGAR.
Edition limited to 185 copies.

34. Tudor Writers on Husbandry.

By Bro. ERNEST CLARKE, F.S.A., Yeoman to the Sette of Odd
Volumes. Read. a Meeting of the Sette held at Limmer's
Hotel, on Friday, February 2nd, 1894.   *In the press.*

35. The Early History of the Royal Society.

By Bro. HENRY B. WHEATLEY, F.S.A., Recorder to the Sette
of Odd Volumes. Read at a Meeting of the Sette held at
Limmer's Hotel, on Friday, November 2nd, 1894.
In the press.

36. An Essay upon Essays.

Written by command of His Oddship Bro. FRANCIS ELGAR
(whom God preserve) and read before the Sette of Odd
Volumes, January 4th, 1895, by Bro. JOHN TODHUNTER, Play-
wright to the Sette. Presented to the Sette by Bro. JOHN
LANE, Bibliographer, at the February Meeting, 1896. (pp. 55.)
Edition limited to 350 copies.

37. Chinese Snuff Bottles of Stone, Porcelain, and Glass, Utilized to Uprear a Fabric of Fancies concerning China and the Chinese.

By Bro. MARCUS B. HUISH, LL.B., M.J.S., Arts-man to the
Sette of Odd Volumes. Delivered at a Meeting of the Sette
held at Limmer's Hotel, on Friday, February 1st, 1895.
(pp. 52.)   Edition limited to 149 copies.

38. Some Words on Allegory in Englaud.

Read to the Odd Volumes at their Meeting, July 5th, 1895, by
their Brother Ignoramus. (pp. 42.)

39. Some Ideal Aspects of the Collector.

By Bro. LE GALLIENNE. Friday, 3rd May, 1895.
In the press.

40. A Potpourri of London Antiquities.

By Bro. Sir STUART KNILL, BART.   Friday, 7th June, 1895.
In the press.

41. Harmonies in Japanese Music.

By Bro. PAUL BEVAN, M.A., Ready Reckoner, Treasurer, and
sometime Secretary to the Sette of Odd Volumes.   Delivered
after Dinner at Limmer's Hotel, on the occasion of the Ladies'
Night, Friday, November 1st, 1895.   Presented to the Sette
by Bro. PAUL BEVAN.   (pp. 70.)
Edition limited to 169 copies.

**42. Ye Minutes of Ye 177th Meeting of Ye Sette
of Odd Volumes.**

Extracted from Ye Diary of SAMUEL PEPYS, Esq., M.A., F.R.S.
Transcribed by Bro. JOHN TODHUNTER, Playwright to Ye Sette.
Privately printed for Ye Sette by ye Hand of their well-beloved
Brother, Ye Chapman.   (pp. 30.)
Edition limited to 154 copies.

Miscellanies.

1. Inaugural Address

of His Oddship, W. M. Thompson, Fourth President of the Sette of Odd Volumes, delivered at the Freemasons' Tavern, Great Queen Street, on his taking office on April 13th, 1883, &c. (pp. 31.) Printed by order of Ye Sette, and issued on May the 4th, 1883.   Edition limited to 250 copies.

2. Codex Chiromantiae.

Appendix A. Dactylomancy, or Finger-ring Magic, Ancient, Mediæval, and Modern. (pp. 34.) Presented on October the 12th, 1883, by Bro. Ed. Heron-Allen.
Edition limited to 153 copies.

3. A President's Persiflage.

Spoken by His Oddship, W. M. Thompson, Fourth President of the Sette of Odd Volumes, at the Freemasons' Tavern, Great Queen Street, at the Fifty-eighth Meeting of the Sette, on December 7th, 1883. (pp. 15.)
Edition limited to 250 copies.

4. Inaugural Address

of His Oddship, Edward F. Wyman, Fifth President of the Sette of Odd Volumes, delivered at the Freemasons' Tavern, Great Queen Street, on his taking office on April 4th, 1884, &c. (pp. 56.) Presented to the Sette by His Oddship Edward F. Wyman.   Edition limited to 133 copies.

5. Musical London a Century Ago.

Compiled from the Raw Material, by Brother Burnham W. Horner, F.R.S.L., F.R.Hist.S., Organist of the Sette of Odd Volumes, delivered at the Freemasons' Tavern, Great Queen Street, on June 6th, 1884. (pp. 32.) Presented to the Sette by His Oddship Edward W. Wyman.
Edition limited to 133 copies

6. The Unfinished Renaissance ;

Or, Fifty Years of English Art. By Bro. GEORGE C. HAITÉ, Author of "Plant Studies," &c. Delivered at the Freemasons' Tavern, Friday, July 11th, 1884. (pp. 40.) Presented to the Sette by His Oddship EDWARD F. WYMAN.

Edition limited to 133 copies.

7. The Pre-Shakespearian Drama.

By Bro. FRANK IRESON. Delivered at the Freemasons' Tavern, Friday, January 2nd, 1885. (pp. 34.) Presented to the Sette by His Oddship EDWARD F. WYMAN.

Edition limited to 133 copies.

8. Inaugural Address

of His Oddship, Brother JAMES ROBERTS BROWN, Sixth President of the Sette of Odd Volumes, delivered at the Freemasons' Tavern, Great Queen Street, on his taking office on April 17th, 1885, &c. (pp. 56.) Presented to the Sette by His Oddship JAMES ROBERTS BROWN.

Edition limited to 133 copies.

9. Catalogue of Works of Art

Exhibited at the Freemasons' Tavern, Great Queen Street, on Friday, July 11th, 1884. Lent by Members of the Sette of Odd Volumes. Presented to the Sette by His Oddship EDWARD F. WYMAN. Edition limited to 255 copies.

10. Catalogue of Manuscripts and Early-Printed Books

Exhibited and Described by Bro. B. QUARITCH, the Librarian of the Sette of Odd Volumes, at the Freemasons' Tavern, Great Queen Street, June 5th, 1885. Presented to the Sette by His Oddship JAMES ROBERTS BROWN.

Edition limited to 255 copies.

11. Catalogue of Old Organ Music

Exhibited by Bro. BURNHAM W. HORNER, F.R.S.L., F.R.Hist.S., Organist of the Sette of Odd Volumes, at the Freemasons' Tavern, Great Queen Street, on Friday, February 5th, 1886. Presented to the Sette by His Oddship JAMES ROBERTS BROWN. Edition limited to 133 copies.

G

12. Inaugural Address

of His Oddship, Bro. GEORGE CLULOW, Seventh President of the Sette of Odd Volumes, delivered at the Freemasons' Tavern, Great Queen Street, on his taking office on April 2nd, 1886, &c. (pp. 64.) Presented to the Sette by His Oddship GEORGE CLULOW. Edition limited to 133 copies.

13. A Few Notes about Arabs.

By Bro. CHARLES HOLME, Pilgrim of the Sette of Odd Volumes. Read at a Meeting of the "Sette" at Willis's Rooms, on Friday, May 7th, 1886. (pp. 46.) Presented to the Sette of Odd Volumes by Bro. CHAS. HOLME.
Edition limited to 133 copies.

14. Account of the Great Learned Societies and Associations, and of the Chief Printing Clubs of Great Britain and Ireland.

Delivered by Bro. BERNARD QUARITCH, Librarian of the Sette of Odd Volumes, at Willis's Rooms, on Tuesday, June 8th, 1886. (pp. 66.) Presented to the Sette by His Oddship GEORGE CLULOW. Edition limited to 255 copies.

15. Report of a Conversazione

Given at Willis's Rooms, King Street, St. James's, on Tuesday, June 8th, 1886, by His Oddship Bro. GEORGE CLULOW, President; with a summary of an Address on "LEARNED SOCIETIES AND PRINTING CLUBS," then delivered by Bro. BERNARD QUARITCH, Librarian. By Bro. W. M. THOMPSON, Historiographer. Presented to the Sette by His Oddship GEORGE CLULOW. Edition limited to 255 copies.

16. Codex Chiromantiae.

Appendix B. A DISCOURSE CONCERNING AUTOGRAPHS AND THEIR SIGNIFICATIONS. Spoken in valediction at Willis's Rooms, on October the 8th, 1886, by Bro. EDWARD HERON-ALLEN. (pp. 45.) Presented to the Sette by His Oddship GEORGE CLULOW. Edition limited to 133 copies.

17. Inaugural Address

of His Oddship, ALFRED J. DAVIES, Eighth President of the Sette of Odd Volumes, delivered at Willis's Rooms, on his taking office on April 4th, 1887. (pp. 64.) Presented to the Sette by His Oddship ALFRED J. DAVIES.

Edition limited to 133 copies.

18. Inaugural Address

of His Oddship, Bro. T. C. VENABLES, Ninth President of the Sette of Odd Volumes, delivered at Willis's Rooms, on his taking office on April 6th, 1888. (pp. 54.) Presented to the Sette by His Oddship T. C. VENABLES.

Edition limithd to 133 copies.

19. Ye Papyrus Roll-Scroll of Ye Sette of Odd Volumes.

By Bro. J. BRODIE-INNES, Master of the Rolls to the Sette of Odd Volumes, delivered at Willis's Rooms, May 4th, 1888. (pp. 39.) Presented to the Sette by His Oddship T. C. VENABLES.

Edition limited to 133 copies.

20. Inaugural Address

of His Oddship, Bro. H. J. GORDON ROSS, Tenth President of the Sette of Odd Volumes, delivered at Willis's Rooms, King Street, St. James's Square, on his taking office, April 5th, 1889.

Edition limited to 255 copies.

SERIES CLOSED.

WORKS DEDICATED TO THE SETTE.

The Ancestry of the Violin.
London, 1882. EDWARD HERON-ALLEN.

An Odd Volume for Smokers.
London, 1889. WALTER HAMILTON.

The Blue Friars.
London, 1889. W. H. K. WRIGHT.

Quatrains.
London, 1892. W. WILSEY MARTIN.

Palæography.
Notes upon the History of Writing, and the Medieval Art o
Illumination.
London, 1894. BERNARD QUARITCH.

The Lay of the Odd Volumes.
Words by W. WILSEY MARTIN.   Music by PAUL BEVAN.
London, 1895.

The Odd Polka.
London, 1895. Music by PAUL BEVAN.

Year-Bokes.

I. The Year-Boke of the Odd Volumes : An Annual Record of the Transactions of the Sette. Eleventh Year, 1888-9.

Written and compiled by Bro. W. MORT THOMPSON, Historiographer to the Sette. Issued November 29th, 1890.

Edition limited to 205 copies.

II. The Year-Boke of the Odd Volumes : An Annual Record of the Transactions of the Sette. Twelfth Year, 1889-90.

Edition limited to 99 copies.

III. The Year-Boke of the Odd Volumes : An Annual Record of the Transactions of the Sette. Thirteenth Year, 1890-91.

Edition limited to 133 copies.

IV. The Year-Boke of the Odd Volumes : An Annual Record of the Transactions of the Sette. Fourteenth Year, 1891-92.

Edition limited to 133 copies.

V. The Year-Boke of the Odd Volumes : An Annual Record of the Transactions of the Sette. Fifteenth Year, 1892-93.

Edition limited to 151 copies.

VI. The Year-Boke of the Odd Volumes : An Annual Record of the Transactions of the Sette. Sixteenth Year, 1893-94.

Written and Compiled by Bro. W. MORT THOMPSON, Historiographer to the Sette. Issued 1895.

Edition limited to 133 copies.

VII. The Year-Boke of the Odd Volumes : An Annual Record of the Transactions of the Sette. Seventeenth Year, 1894-95.

Edited by Bro. WILLIAM MANNING, Seer to the Sette. Issued 1897.

Edition limited to 149 copies.

Folia.

ORIGINATED BY BRO. HOLME, *Pilgrim*, WHO PRESENTED
EACH·BROTHER WITH A SPECIAL PORTFOLIO.

1. ## The Victualling Crew.
   Presented by Bro. HENRY MOORE, R.A., *Ancient Mariner*.
   Feb. 6th, 1891.

2. ## Proud Maisie.
   From a drawing by Frederick Sandys.   Presented by Bro.
   TODHUNTER, *Playwright*.   Nov. 6th, 1891.

3. ## A Wet Day in Hakone, Japan.
   Presented by Bro. ALFRED EAST, *Landscape Painter*,
   Jan. 8th, 1892.

4. ## The Dead Shelley.
   Presented by BRO. ONSLOW FORD, A.R.A., *Sculptor*. Nov.
   2nd, 1892.

5. ## Moonlight-Twilight on the River Eamont, Cumberland.
   Presented by Bro. HENRY MOORE, R.A., *Ancient Mariner*.

6. ## The Calm Lagoon.
   Presented by Bro. WILFRID BALL, R.E., *Painter Etcher*.
   Feb. 5th, 1897.

Ye BEDFORD PRESS

20 AND 21, BEDFORDBURY,
LONDON, W.C.

www.ingramcontent.com/pod-product-compliance
Lightning Source LLC
Chambersburg PA
CBHW021532270326
41930CB00008B/1219